Team Spirit

THE NEW YORK METS

BY

MARK STEWART

Content Consultant
James L. Gates, Jr.
Library Director
National Baseball Hall of Fame and Museum

NORWOOD HOUSE PRESS
CHICAGO, ILLINOIS

Norwood House Press
P.O. Box 316598
Chicago, Illinois 60631

For information regarding Norwood House Press, please visit our website at:
www.norwoodhousepress.com or call 866-565-2900.

All photos courtesy of AP Images—AP/Wide World Photos, Inc. except the following:
Topps, Inc (7, 9 both, 14, 16, 26 both, 34 left and right & 40 top left and left);
Black Book archives (15, 20, 21 both, 22 both, 23 top, 34 top, 35 all, 39 top & 43);
Sports Stars Publishing (37); Author's Collection (40 bottom).
Special thanks to Topps, Inc.

Editor: Mike Kennedy
Designer: Ron Jaffe
Project Management: Black Book Partners, LLC.
Special thanks to Nancy Volkman and Peter Coan

Library of Congress Cataloging-in-Publication Data

Stewart, Mark, 1960-
    The New York Mets / by Mark Stewart ; with content consultant James L.
Gates, Jr.
        p. cm. -- (Team spirit)
    Summary: "Presents the history, accomplishments and key personalities of
the New York Mets baseball team. Includes timelines, quotes, maps, glossary
and websites"--Provided by publisher.
    Includes bibliographical references and index.
    ISBN-13: 978-1-59953-061-1 (library edition : alk. paper)
    ISBN-10: 1-59953-061-9 (library edition : alk. paper)
    1. New York Mets (Baseball team)--History--Juvenile literature. I. Gates,
Jr., James L. II. Title. III. Series: Stewart, Mark, 1960- Team spirit.
    GV875.N45S74 2007
    796.357'64097471--dc22
                                            2006015331

Manufactured in the United States of America.

9267

COVER PHOTO: The Mets celebrate an exciting win during the 2005 season.

Table of Contents

SPORTS WORDS & VOCABULARY WORDS: In this book, you will find many words that are new to you. You may also see familiar words used in new ways. The glossary on page 46 gives the meanings of baseball words, as well as "everyday" words that have special baseball meanings. These words appear in **bold type** throughout the book. The glossary on page 47 gives the meanings of vocabulary words that are not related to baseball. They appear in ***bold italic type*** throughout the book.

Meet the Mets

As long as baseball has been played, one thing has always been true—you need good pitching and good fielding to win championships. No one knows this better than the New York Mets. Each time they have won a **pennant**, their pitchers and fielders have been the keys to their success.

The Mets are also known for having some of baseball's most *colorful* characters. There must be something about playing in New York that brings out the true personality in a player. This is what the Mets' fans love most of all about their team, and why they are so loyal. The players seem like friends from school or work or the neighborhood. And you never give up on a friend.

This book tells the story of the Mets. Sometimes the team has been very good, and sometimes it has not. Win or lose, however, the Mets have always put on a good show.

The friendly, relaxed manner of young stars
David Wright and Jose Reyes makes them fan favorites.

Way Back When

For a period of more than 80 years, there had been two **National League (N.L.)** teams in New York City—the New York Giants and Brooklyn Dodgers. They had one of baseball's fiercest *rivalries*. In 1958, both teams moved to California. Suddenly, the city's N.L. fans had no one to root for. In 1962, the league added two teams, the Houston Colt .45s and the Metropolitan Baseball Club of New York—better known as the New York Mets.

In their early years, the Mets played right across the river from the New York Yankees, who were champions of the **American League (A.L.)**. In order to *attract* fans, the Mets used players who had once been stars for the city's other teams. These players included Gil Hodges, Duke Snider, Charlie Neal, Roger Craig, Gene Woodling, Tom Sturdivant, and Clem Labine. Their manager was Casey Stengel, who had been a member of the Giants, Dodgers, and Yankees.

Gil Hodges and Duke Snider played together on the Brooklyn Dodgers during the 1940s and 1950s. Both joined the Mets in 1962.

Casey Stengel watches his players practice on this 1964 baseball card. The team lost more than 100 games that season.

CASEY STENGEL   Manager

Other Mets who were familiar to old-time baseball fans were Richie Ashburn, Frank Thomas, Gus Bell, George Altman, Roy McMillan, and Carlton Willey. Unfortunately, these players were no longer stars when they joined the team. The Mets made a lot of mistakes, and did not win very often.

Even though the Mets usually lost, millions of fans still came to see them. The team made a lot of money, and spent it *developing* young players who could help them win. The Mets won the pennant and **World Series** in 1969. The team's pitchers were the best in baseball. The Mets' **pitching staff** included Tom Seaver, Jerry Koosman, Gary Gentry, Nolan Ryan, and Tug McGraw. Their best defensive players were Jerry Grote, Bud Harrelson, Tommie Agee, and Cleon Jones.

The Mets added more good players over the next few years, including Jon Matlack, John Milner, Rusty Staub, Felix Millan, and Willie Mays. They won the pennant again in 1973, but lost the World Series.

By the end of the 1970s, Seaver and the team's other stars had either been traded or had retired. Many years passed before the Mets put another good team on the field. Once again, they built their club around a group of young pitchers, led by Dwight Gooden, Ron Darling, Sid Fernandez, Jesse Orosco, and Roger McDowell. The team starred **veterans** Gary Carter, Keith Hernandez, and Ray Knight, as well as exciting young players Darryl Strawberry, Lenny Dykstra, and Mookie Wilson. In 1986, the Mets won their third pennant and second World Series.

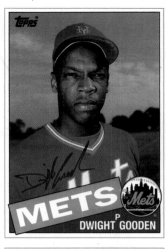

In 2000, the Mets returned to the World Series. They were led by pitchers Mike Hampton, Al Leiter, John Franco, and Armando Benitez. The Mets had one of the best-fielding teams ever. Their **offense** was led by Mike Piazza and Edgardo Alfonzo.

The Mets played the Yankees for the championship that fall. It was the first time New York teams had met in the World Series since 1956. Even though the Mets lost, they reminded baseball fans everywhere of the "good old days," when the city was the center of baseball almost every autumn.

RIGHT: Dwight Gooden and Darryl Strawberry, the young stars who led the Mets in the 1980s.   **LEFT**: Tom Seaver, whose pitching helped the Mets win two pennants.

The Team Today

The Mets like to bring exciting players to the ballpark each year. They are not afraid to change with the times, even if it means rebuilding their entire team. More than two million fans come to the stadium each season, hoping that this will be the year that they return to the World Series.

In 2004, the Mets hired Omar Minaya to be their *general manager*. His job was to put together a championship **lineup**. Minaya was one of the first Latinos to run a **major-league** baseball team. With his help, the Mets were able to create a clubhouse where players from many different cultures could feel welcome. Suddenly, many of baseball's best Spanish-speaking stars wanted to play in New York—including Pedro Martinez, Carlos Beltran, and Carlos Delgado.

These **All-Stars** used their talent and experience to help New York's younger players, including Jose Reyes and David Wright, who also became stars. With good pitching and fielding, the Mets always have their eye on the World Series.

Carlos Delgado and Carlos Beltran share a joke near the batting cage.

Home Turf

In 1964, the Mets moved into brand new Shea Stadium. It opened at the same time as the New York World's Fair, in the **borough** of Queens. The stadium was named after William Shea, a man who worked very hard to bring National League baseball back to New York after the Dodgers and Giants left town. The seats at Shea Stadium are a reminder of these teams. They have always been Dodger blue and Giant orange.

One of the first things fans noticed about Shea Stadium was how noisy it was on certain days. This is because one of the world's busiest airports is located nearby. When the wind blows in a certain direction, the planes take off right over the ballpark!

The Mets plan to open a new stadium for the 2009 season. It will be a mix of old-time **architecture** and modern technology. It will be located next to Shea Stadium.

SHEA STADIUM BY THE NUMBERS

- *Shea Stadium cost $25.5 million to build in the early 1960s.*
- *The distance from home plate to the left field foul pole is 338 feet.*
- *The distance from home plate to the right field foul pole is 338 feet.*
- *The distance from home plate to the center field fence is 410 feet.*

The teams line up for a 2000 World Series game at Shea Stadium.

Dressed for Success

Since the very first day they took the field, the Mets have worn the blue of the Dodgers and the orange of the Giants. They wanted the fans of these old New York teams to see familiar colors when they came to the ballpark.

The team *logo* features the New York skyline inside of a baseball. It was designed by a cartoonist named Ray Gatto. If you look carefully, you can see the Empire State Building, the United Nations Building, and the Williamsburg Savings Bank, which is the tallest building in Brooklyn.

The team has worn different shades and combinations of orange, blue, and white over the years. When the Mets play at home, they often use a *pinstriped* uniform that is almost identical to the one they wore in 1962. It is still the fans' favorite.

Charlie Smith wears the team's 1964 uniform. The Mets wore a special New York World's Fair patch on their sleeves that year.

UNIFORM BASICS

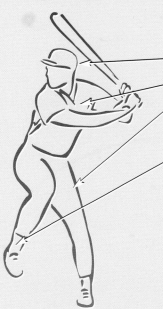

The baseball uniform has not changed much since the Mets began playing. It has four main parts:

- a cap or batting helmet with a sun visor;
- a top with a player's number on the back;
- pants that reach down between the ankle and the knee;
- stirrup-style socks.

The uniform top sometimes has a player's name on the back. The team's name, city, or logo is usually on the front. Baseball teams wear light-colored uniforms when they play at home, and darker styles when they play on the road.

For more than 100 years, baseball uniforms were made of wool *flannel* and were very baggy. This helped the sweat *evaporate* and gave players the freedom to move around. Today's uniforms are made of *synthetic* fabrics that stretch with players and keep them dry and cool.

Aaron Heilman throws a pitch wearing the team's "classic" home uniform.

We Won!

When the Mets are playing for a championship, baseball fans have come to expect the unexpected. In 1969, for example, few people in baseball believed they would win more than half their games when the season started. What were the chances of winning the World Series? Well, the Mets had never even had a winning *year*. It seemed impossible.

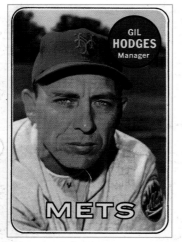

One person who believed in the Mets was their manager, Gil Hodges. He had played in seven World Series, and knew exactly what it took to get there. He promised his players that if they simply made fewer mistakes than their opponents, then they would have a chance.

The Mets were led by pitchers Tom Seaver and Jerry Koosman. They were very young and very good. Seaver won 25 games and Koosman won 17. They did not have many good hitters, but they made the most of their chances while batting and played well in the field. Hodges was very good at guessing who would do well each game, and gave everyone a chance to play. At the end of the year, the Mets had won 100 games, and were the champions of the **N.L. East.**

After defeating the hard-hitting Atlanta Braves in the **National League Championship Series (NLCS)**, the Mets faced the Baltimore Orioles in the World Series. The Orioles looked unbeatable. They had won nine more games, scored 147 more runs, and batted 23 points higher than the Mets.

The Mets lost the first game, but in each of the next four games, they managed to make the right play at just the right moment, and beat the Orioles each time. The hitting star of the series was Donn Clendenon, a 35-year-old first baseman who had almost retired earlier in the season. The best fielding play was made by Ron Swoboda, who  was not known for his defense. The team that had once been called the "Amazin' Mets" as a joke amazed the baseball world by beating the mighty Orioles and becoming champions.

LEFT: Gil Hodges **ABOVE**: New York City Mayor John Lindsay joins Tom Seaver as they celebrate a New York pennant.

Seventeen years later, the Mets won their second championship. In many ways, this victory was even *more* amazing. They barely won the pennant, beating the Houston Astros in a wild 16-inning game in the NLCS. Then the Mets lost the first two games of the World Series to the Boston Red Sox—in Shea Stadium. No team had ever won a championship after losing the opening games on their home field.

Led by the pitching of Bob Ojeda and Ron Darling, and the hitting of Lenny Dykstra and Gary Carter, New York battled back to tie the series at three victories each. The Mets almost lost the sixth

game, but made a remarkable comeback to win in the 10th inning. The team had to come from behind again in Game Seven. They won 8–5 on hits by Keith Hernandez, Ray Knight, and Darryl Strawberry. For the second time in the history of Shea Stadium, thousands of fans poured onto the field to celebrate their champion Mets.

LEFT: Lenny Dykstra rounds the bases after hitting a home run to start Game Three of the 1986 World Series. This hit helped the Mets fight their way back after two losses.   **ABOVE**: Ray Knight strokes the winning hit in Game Seven of the 1986 World Series.

Go-To Guys

To be a true star in baseball, you need more than a quick bat and a strong arm. You have to be a "go-to guy"—someone the manager wants on the pitcher's mound or in the batter's box when it matters most. Mets fans have had a lot to cheer about over the years, including these great stars...

THE PIONEERS

TOM SEAVER   Pitcher

• BORN: 11/17/1944 • PLAYED FOR TEAM: 1967 TO 1977 AND 1983

Tom Seaver was the team's first true star. He threw one fastball that hopped as it neared home plate, and another fastball that dipped. Batters did not know which to swing at until it was too late. "Tom Terrific" was an All-Star nine times with the Mets.

JERRY KOOSMAN   Pitcher

• BORN: 12/23/1942

• PLAYED FOR TEAM: 1967 TO 1978

Jerry Koosman had a good fastball, a great curve, and a "**cutter**" that caused a lot of broken bats. He was the pitching star of the 1969 World Series, beating the Orioles in Game Two and Game Five.

KEITH HERNANDEZ   First Baseman

• BORN: 10/20/1953   • PLAYED FOR TEAM: 1983 TO 1989

Keith Hernandez was the best fielder in team history. He won the **Gold Glove** six times in the seven seasons he played for the Mets. Hernandez was also one of baseball's best **clutch hitters**.

DARRYL STRAWBERRY   Outfielder

• BORN: 3/12/1962   • PLAYED FOR TEAM: 1983 TO 1990

Darryl Strawberry was the first great hitter the Mets developed. He was a tall, graceful athlete with a beautiful swing. Strawberry was an All-Star in seven of his eight seasons with the Mets.

DWIGHT GOODEN   Pitcher

• BORN: 11/16/1964   • PLAYED FOR TEAM: 1984 TO 1994

Dwight Gooden had baseball's best fastball and most amazing curve during the mid 1980s. He struck out 276 batters when he was 19. At age 20, he led the N.L. in wins, strikeouts, and **earned run average (ERA)**.

GARY CARTER   Catcher

• BORN: 4/8/1954   • PLAYED FOR TEAM: 1985 TO 1989

The Mets needed an experienced catcher to work with their young pitchers in the 1980s. In 1985, they traded for Gary Carter, and one year later they were world champions.

LEFT: Jerry Koosman
TOP RIGHT: Darryl Strawberry   **BOTTOM RIGHT**: Gary Carter

JOHN FRANCO **Pitcher**

- Born: 9/17/1960 • Played for Team: 1990 to 2004

John Franco's job was to slam the door on opponents in the ninth inning and save the game for the Mets. He did this 276 times for the team, and led the N.L. in **saves** twice while pitching in New York.

MIKE PIAZZA **Catcher**

- Born: 9/4/1968
- Played for Team: 1998 to 2005

Mike Piazza ranks among the greatest hitting catchers in baseball history. When the Mets won the pennant in 2000, he led all catchers in batting average, home runs, and fielding percentage.

TOM GLAVINE **Pitcher**

- Born: 3/25/1966
- First Year with Team: 2003

Tom Glavine beat the Mets year after year when he pitched for their rivals, the Atlanta Braves. When they had a chance to sign him in 2003, they did!

JOSE REYES   Shortstop

- BORN: 6/11/1983
- FIRST YEAR WITH TEAM: 2003

Shea Stadium began buzzing with excitement the first day Jose Reyes stepped on the field. His tremendous speed, powerful arm, and lively bat made him one of the best shortstops ever to wear a Mets uniform.

DAVID WRIGHT   Third Baseman

- BORN: 12/20/1982
- FIRST YEAR WITH TEAM: 2004

The Mets searched many years for a star to play third base for them. Their search ended when power-hitting David Wright joined the team.

PEDRO MARTINEZ   Pitcher

- BORN: 10/25/1971
- FIRST YEAR WITH TEAM: 2005

The Mets needed a pitcher who could win close games and also be a leader in the clubhouse. They **entrusted** this job to Pedro Martinez, and he quickly became the team's most admired player.

TOP LEFT: Mike Piazza   **TOP RIGHT**: Jose Reyes
BOTTOM LEFT: Tom Glavine   **BOTTOM RIGHT**: David Wright

On the Sidelines

The Mets have always liked to hire "hometown guys" to run the team. Their first manager, Casey Stengel, had played and managed in New York since 1912. Gil Hodges and Yogi Berra—who each led the Mets to a pennant—had been New York baseball heroes since the 1940s. Other Mets managers who either grew up or played in New York included Wes Westrum, Joe Torre, George Bamberger, and Bobby Valentine.

One of the team's best managers was Davey Johnson, who was not a New Yorker. He was hired in 1984, and the Mets finished first or second in the N.L. East every year he managed them. Johnson demanded that his players give him a full effort every second they were on the field. Teams could never take it easy against the Mets when Johnson was in charge.

In 2004, the Mets hired another hometown hero, Willie Randolph. Randolph had been an All-Star many times with the Yankees. He also played for the Mets. Randolph won 11 pennants as a coach and manager before coming to the Mets, and brought this winning *tradition* to the New York dugout.

Willie Randolph has played, coached, and managed in New York.

One Great Day

Game Six of the 1986 World Series will forever be remembered as the most amazing day in Mets history. The Boston Red Sox led the series three games to two. As the bottom of the 10th inning began, the Mets were losing 5–3. There were only three outs left in their season.

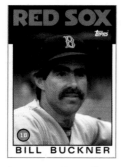

RED SOX

BILL BUCKNER

METS

MOOKIE WILSON

Boston got two of those outs quickly, and then two strikes on the next batter, Gary Carter. The Red Sox players inched closer to the top step of their dugout, waiting for that moment when they could run onto the field and start celebrating. But Carter hit a single to keep New York's hopes alive. Then Kevin Mitchell singled. Ray Knight was next. He hit a single with two strikes, and Carter scored to make it 5–4.

Relief pitcher Bob Stanley came into the game to pitch to Mookie Wilson. After getting two strikes on Wilson, he tried to put a little too much on a pitch and it sailed way inside. Wilson jumped out of the way and the ball rolled to the **backstop**. Mitchell scored the tying run, and Knight ran to second base.

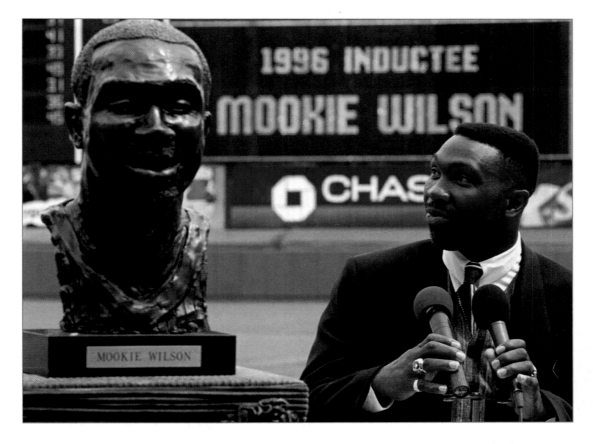

The next pitch was a good, low strike. Wilson pounded it into the ground, and it rolled toward Bill Buckner, the first baseman. Worried that the speedy Wilson might beat him to the base, Buckner took his eye off the ball for an instant—and it rolled under his glove and into the outfield. Knight scored all the way from second base to win the game! The Mets then beat Boston in Game Seven to win the world championship.

ABOVE: Mookie Wilson is honored at Shea Stadium 10 years after his famous hit against the Red Sox.   **LEFT**: When Bill Buckner and Mookie Wilson posed for their 1986 trading cards, they had no idea that they would one day share an historic baseball moment.

Legend Has It

Who once ran the bases backwards for the Mets?

LEGEND HAS IT Jimmy Piersall did. In 1963, Piersall joined the Mets with 99 career home runs. He decided to make number 100 a hit to remember. After blasting the ball over the fence against the Philadelphia Phillies, Piersall turned around and ***backpedaled*** his way around the bases. After rounding third base, he slid into home plate backwards.

How did John Franco learn to pitch under pressure?

LEGEND HAS IT that he learned playing Wiffle Ball. Franco and his older brother grew up in Brooklyn, and played one-on-one Wiffle Ball games all summer. His brother would let him get way ahead, then come back to beat him in the last inning. After years of these frustrating defeats, Franco finally learned how to "close" games against his brother. A few years later, he was using the same tricks to close major-league games!

What caused the strangest game delay in team history?

LEGEND HAS IT that a computer was to blame. The Mets have had games interrupted for many reasons, including a black cat running across the field, a bird hit by a batted ball, fans jumping out of the stands, and the New York City *blackout* of 1977. Nothing was stranger, however, than what happened in the first inning of a 2005 game against the Arizona Diamondbacks. Pedro Martinez

was on the mound when suddenly the Shea Stadium sprinkler system was *activated*. Everyone ran off the field except Martinez. He thought it was the funniest thing he had ever seen.

LEFT: Jimmy Piersall prepares to slide into home—backwards. This was the only home run he hit for the Mets. Piersall was soon traded.
RIGHT: All Pedro Martinez can do is laugh when the sprinklers come on during his start against the Diamondbacks.

It Really Happened

You can never count the Mets out. They have proved this again and again during their history. During the summer of 1973, everyone in baseball thought New York's season was over. On August 17th, the Mets were in last place in the N.L. East. Five of their best players—Bud Harrelson, Jerry Grote, Cleon Jones, John Milner, and Willie Mays—had been hurt for much of the season.

When these players returned to the lineup, the Mets started winning. Slowly but surely, they began passing the clubs in front of them. Could the Mets do the impossible? Tug McGraw, the team's star relief pitcher, kept saying "You gotta believe." Soon, YOU GOTTA BELIEVE buttons and signs started popping up all over the city.

On September 27th, New York fans woke up to find their team in first place. On October 1st, Jon Matlack pitched a two-hitter against the Chicago Cubs to give the Mets the N.L. East title. They finished with 82 wins, one more than the second-place St. Louis Cardinals. The Mets went on to beat the Cincinnati Reds in the playoffs and win the pennant. In just a few weeks, New York had gone from worst to first!

Willie Mays, in his final year as a player, enjoys his team's amazing victory.

Team Spirit

The "Amazing Mets" have always been famous for their amazing fans. When the team was losing 100 games a year during the 1960s, they often had bigger crowds than New York's other team, the champion Yankees. This drove the Yankees crazy! During those early years, many great traditions started. They include days when the fans are allowed to run the bases, and days when they compete to see who can make the best *banner*.

The Mets may be the only team that has had the same cheer for more than 40 years. Since that first season back in 1962, fans have been chanting "Let's Go Mets!" at every game.

Something else that has happened at every Mets game since 1962 is a visit from Mr. Met. The team's mascot has a wide smile and a gigantic baseball-shaped head. He walks through the crowd and shakes hands, leads cheers, and sometimes dances on top of the dugout.

You do not have to be a kid to love Mr. Met. He has been coming to Mets games since the fans in this picture were small children.

Timeline

Jon Matlack

1962
The Mets play their first season and lose a record 120 games.

1967
Tom Seaver is named N.L. **Rookie of the Year**.

1972
Jon Matlack is named N.L. Rookie of the Year.

1964
Ron Hunt becomes the first Met to start in the All-Star Game.

1969
The Mets defeat the Baltimore Orioles in the World Series.

1964 ALL STARS

RON HUNT

Ron Hunt

Tom Seaver, who won 25 games for the 1969 Mets.

METS

Tom Seaver | PITCHER

Yogi
Berra

2000
The Mets win
their fourth
pennant and play
the Yankees in a
"Subway Series."

1973
Yogi Berra manages
the Mets to the N.L.
pennant.

1986
The Mets defeat the Boston Red
Sox to win their second World Series.

1984
Dwight Gooden is named
N.L. Rookie of the Year.

1991
David Cone
leads the N.L.
in strikeouts
for the second
year in a row.

2005
Jose Reyes leads the N.L.
with 60 stolen bases.

David
Cone

Jose
Reyes

Fun Facts

YOU BIG APE!

The most powerful hitter in Mets history was Dave Kingman. He slugged several 500-foot home runs, and could hit balls over the fence on one-handed swings. Kingman's nickname was "Kong."

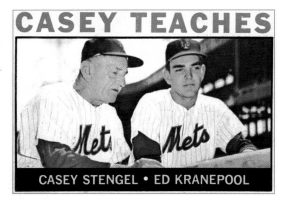

CASEY TEACHES

CASEY STENGEL • ED KRANEPOOL

THE GRADUATE

In 1962, 17-year-old Ed Kranepool graduated from high school in New York and was playing first base for the Mets a few weeks later.

WORKING LATE

In April of 1968, the Mets lost to the Houston Astros 1–0 in a game that lasted six hours and six minutes. The only run was scored on an error by New York shortstop Al Weis in the 24th inning.

SHARP GUY

Mets center fielder Lenny Dykstra was so tough and *intense* that teammates called him "Nails."

PACIFIC HEIGHTS

The Mets have had great luck with players born in Hawaii, Japan, and Korea. Among the most successful were Sid Fernandez, Ron Darling, Benny Agbayani, Jae Weong Seo, Dae-Sung Koo, Hideo Nomo, Kazuhisa Ishii, Shingo Takatsu, Kazuo Matsui, Masato Yoshii, and Tsuyoshi Shinjo.

A MAN OF TASTE

Outfielder Rusty Staub was the best hitter on the 1973 Mets—and the best cook. Staub was a trained chef who owned his own restaurant.

LIGHTS OUT

On July 25, 1977, thousands of fans at Shea Stadium were left in the dark when a blackout struck New York City. To help the fans find their way, the players drove their cars onto the field and shone their headlights into the stands.

ABOVE: Rusty Staub
LEFT: Old-timer Casey Stengel talks hitting with teenager Ed Kranepool.

Talking Baseball

"Baseball is a game of the soul."
—*Pedro Martinez, on what makes baseball different from other sports*

"I'm going to stop saying 'I've seen it all.'
Because every time I do, something else crazy happens."
—*Willie Randolph, on the unpredictable side of baseball*

TOP RIGHT: Cliff Floyd   **BOTTOM RIGHT**: David Wright
ABOVE: Omar Minaya and Willie Randolph pose with pitcher Pedro Martinez.

"I always dreamed of one day playing in New York. Now that dream has finally come true."
—*Cliff Floyd, on why he signed to play with the Mets*

"If you don't think baseball is a big deal, don't do it. But if you do it, do it *right*."
—*Tom Seaver, on learning the fundamentals*

"I love being a Met. It was my favorite team growing up, so to be a Met, to me, is very special."
—*David Wright, on realizing his childhood dream*

"Can't anybody here play this game?!"
—*Casey Stengel, on the frustrating 1962 Mets*

For the Record

The great Mets teams and players have left their marks on the record books. These are the "best of the best"…

METS AWARD WINNERS

WINNER	AWARD	YEAR
Tom Seaver	Rookie of the Year	1967
Tom Seaver	Cy Young Award*	1969
Donn Clendenon	World Series Most Valuable Player	1969
Jon Matlack	Rookie of the Year	1972
Tom Seaver	Cy Young Award	1973
Tom Seaver	Cy Young Award	1975
Darryl Strawberry	Rookie of the Year	1983
Dwight Gooden	Rookie of the Year	1984
Dwight Gooden	Cy Young Award	1985
Ray Knight	World Series Most Valuable Player	1986
John Franco	Reliever of the Year	1990
Armando Benitez	Reliever of the Year	2001

The Cy Young Award is given to the league's best pitcher each year.

Donn Clendenon 1ST BASE

DARRYL STRAWBERRY OF

TOP: Donn Clendenon
ABOVE: Darryl Strawberry
RIGHT: A souvenir photo of the 1969 Mets.

WORLD CHAMPION NEW YORK METS

FRONT ROW (left to right)—Ex-Trainer Gus Mauch, coach Joe Pignatano, coach Rube Walker, coach Yogi Berra, coach Eddie Yost, assistant trainer Joe Deer.
SECOND ROW—Tug McGraw, Gary Gentry, Al Weis, Cleon Jones, Manager Gil Hodges, Jerry Grote, Bud Harrelson, Ed Charles, Rod Gaspar, Duffy Dyer.
THIRD ROW—Jim McAndrew, Tommie Agee, Cal Koonce, Ken Boswell, Tom Seaver, Jerry Koosman, Ron Swoboda, Wayne Garrett, Bobby Pfeil, traveling Sec. Lou Niss.
BACK ROW—Equip. Mgr. Nick Torman, J. C. Martin, Ron Taylor, Ed Kranepool, Don Cardwell, Donn Clendenon, Nolan Ryan, Art Shamsky, Jack DiLauro, clubhouse attendant Roy Neuer.

METS ACHIEVEMENTS

ACHIEVEMENT	YEAR
N.L. East Champions	1969
N.L. Pennant Winners	1969
World Series Champions	1969
N.L. East Champions	1973
N.L. Pennant Winners	1973
N.L. East Champions	1986
N.L. Pennant Winners	1986
World Series Champions	1986
N.L. East Champions	1988
N.L. Pennant Winners	2000
N.L. East Champions	2006

TOP: Ray Knight and Gary Carter celebrate the team's victory in 1986.
ABOVE: The celebration begins after the final out of the 1969 World Series.
LEFT: John Franco waves to the fans after the Mets win the 2000 pennant.

Pinpoints

The history of a baseball team is made up of many smaller stories. These stories take place all over the map—not just in the city a team calls "home." Match the push-pins on these maps to the Team Facts and you will begin to see the story of the Mets unfold!

TEAM FACTS

1 Flushing, New York—*The Mets play here.*

2 Fresno, California—*Tom Seaver was born here.*

3 Tampa, Florida—*Dwight Gooden was born here.*

4 Norfolk, Virginia—*David Wright was born here.*

5 Pendleton, Oregon—*Dave Kingman was born here.*

6 Concord, Massachusetts—*Tom Glavine was born here.*

7 Appleton, Minnesota—*Jerry Koosman was born here.*

8 Norristown, Pennsylvania—*Mike Piazza was born here.*

9 Honolulu, Hawaii—*Sid Fernandez was born here.*

10 Fukuoka, Japan—*Tsuyoshi Shinjo was born here.*

11 Manati, Puerto Rico—*Carlos Beltran was born here.*

12 Villa Gonzalez, Dominican Republic—
Jose Reyes was born here.

Tsuyoshi Shinjo

43

Play Ball

Baseball is a game played between two teams over nine innings. Teams take one turn at bat and one turn in the field during each inning. A turn at bat ends when three outs are made. The batters on the hitting team try to reach base safely. The players on the fielding team try to prevent this from happening.

In baseball, the ball is controlled by the pitcher. The pitcher must throw the ball to the batter, who decides whether or not to swing at each pitch. If a batter swings and misses, it is a strike. If the batter lets a good pitch go by, it is also a strike. If the batter swings and the ball does not stay in fair territory (between the v-shaped lines that begin at home plate) it is called "foul," and is counted as a strike. If the pitcher throws three strikes, the batter is out. If the pitcher throws four bad pitches before that, the batter is awarded first base. This is called a base-on-balls, or "walk."

When the batter swings the bat and hits the ball, everyone springs into action. If a fielder catches a batted ball before it hits the ground, the batter is out. If a fielder scoops the ball off the ground and throws it to first base before the batter arrives, the batter is out. If the batter reaches first base safely, he is credited with a hit. A one-base hit is called a single, a two-base hit is called a double, a three-base hit is called a triple, and a four-base hit is called a home run.

Runners who reach base are only safe when they are touching one of the bases. If they are caught between the bases, the fielders can tag them with the ball and record an out.

A batter who is able to circle the bases and make it back to home plate before three outs are made is credited with a run scored. The team with the most runs after nine innings is the winner.

Anyone who has played baseball (or softball) knows that it can be a complicated game. Every player on the field has a job to do. Different players have different strengths and weaknesses. The pitchers, batters, and managers make hundreds of decisions every game. The more you play and watch baseball, the more "little things" you are likely to notice. The next time you are at a game, look for these plays:

PLAY LIST

DOUBLE PLAY—A play where the fielding team is able to make two outs on one batted ball. This usually happens when a runner is on first base, and the batter hits a ground ball to one of the infielders. The base runner is forced out at second base and the ball is then thrown to first base before the batter arrives.

HIT AND RUN—A play where the runner on first base sprints to second base while the pitcher is throwing the ball to the batter. When the second baseman or shortstop moves toward the base to wait for the catcher's throw, the batter tries to hit the ball to the place that the fielder has just left. If the batter swings and misses, the fielding team can tag the runner out.

INTENTIONAL WALK—A play when the pitcher throws four bad pitches on purpose, allowing the batter to walk to first base. This happens when the pitcher would much rather face the next batter—and is willing to risk putting a runner on base.

SACRIFICE BUNT—A play where the batter makes an out on purpose so that a teammate can move to the next base. On a bunt, the batter tries to "deaden" the pitch with the bat instead of swinging at it.

SHOESTRING CATCH—A play where an outfielder catches a short hit an inch or two above the ground, near the tops of his shoes. It is not easy to run as fast as you can and lower your glove without slowing down. It can be risky, too. If a fielder misses a shoestring catch, the ball might roll all the way to the fence.

Glossary

BASEBALL WORDS TO KNOW

ALL-STARS—Players who are selected to play in baseball's annual All-Star Game.

AMERICAN LEAGUE (A.L.)—One of baseball's two major leagues. The A.L. started play in 1901.

BACKSTOP—The wall or fence behind home plate.

CLUTCH HITTERS—Hitters who do well under pressure, or "in the clutch."

CUTTER—A fastball that is curved slightly by spinning it sideways.

EARNED RUN AVERAGE (ERA)—A statistic that measures how many runs a pitcher gives up for every nine innings he pitches.

GOLD GLOVE—An award given each year to baseball's best fielders.

LINEUP—The list of players who are playing in a game.

MAJOR-LEAGUE—Belonging to the American or National League, which make up the major leagues.

NATIONAL LEAGUE (N.L.)—The older of the two major leagues. The N.L. started play in 1876.

NATIONAL LEAGUE CHAMPIONSHIP SERIES (NLCS)—The competition that has decided the National League pennant since 1969.

N.L. EAST—A group of National League teams that play in the eastern part of the country.

OFFENSE—The players who help a team score runs.

PENNANT—A league championship. The term comes from the triangular flag awarded to each season's champion, beginning in the 1870s.

PITCHING STAFF—The group of players who pitch for a team.

ROOKIE OF THE YEAR—An annual award given to each league's best first-year player.

SAVES—A statistic that measures the number of times a relief pitcher finishes off a close victory for his team.

SUBWAY SERIES—A meeting between two teams whose stadiums are connected by a subway.

VETERANS—Players who have great experience.

WORLD SERIES—The world championship series played between the winners of the American and National Leagues.

OTHER WORDS TO KNOW

ACTIVATED—Turned on or put into motion.

ARCHITECTURE—A style of building.

ATTRACT—To get the attention of.

BACKPEDALED—Walked or ran in reverse.

BANNER—A flag with words and pictures.

BLACKOUT—A power failure that causes the lights to go out.

BOROUGH—One of the five cities that make up New York City.

COLORFUL—Lively and interesting.

DEVELOPING—Bringing out the potential in someone or something.

ENTRUSTED—To give someone the responsibility of care and protection.

EVAPORATE—Disappear, or turn into vapor.

FLANNEL—A soft wool or cotton material.

GENERAL MANAGER—A person who oversees all parts of a company.

INTENSE—Very strong or very deep.

LOGO—A symbol or design that represents a company or team.

PINSTRIPED—A design with thin stripes.

RIVALRIES—Extremely emotional competitions.

SYNTHETIC—Made in a laboratory, not in nature.

TRADITION—A belief or custom that is handed down from generation to generation.

Places to Go
ON THE ROAD

SHEA STADIUM
123-01 Roosevelt Avenue
Flushing, New York 11368
(718) 507-6387

**NATIONAL BASEBALL
HALL OF FAME AND MUSEUM**
25 Main Street
Cooperstown, New York 13326
(888) 425-5633
www.baseballhalloffame.org

ON THE WEB

THE NEW YORK METS   www.Mets.com
  • *to learn more about the Mets*

MAJOR LEAGUE BASEBALL   www.mlb.com
  • *to learn about all the major league teams*

MINOR LEAGUE BASEBALL   www.minorleaguebaseball.com
  • *to learn more about the minor leagues*

ON THE BOOKSHELVES

To learn more about the sport of baseball, look for these books at your library or bookstore:

• Kelly, James. *Baseball*. New York, NY: DK, 2005.

• Jacobs, Greg. *The Everything Kids' Baseball Book*. Cincinnati, OH: Adams Media Corporation, 2006.

• Stewart, Mark and Kennedy, Mike. *Long Ball: The Legend and Lore of the Home Run*. Minneapolis, MN: Millbrook Press, 2006.

Index

The Team

MARK STEWART has written more than 25 books on baseball, and over 100 sports books for kids. He grew up in New York City during the 1960s rooting for the Yankees and Mets, and now takes his two daughters, Mariah and Rachel, to the same ballparks. Mark comes from a family of writers. His grandfather was Sunday Editor of The *New York Times* and his mother was Articles Editor of *Ladies Home Journal* and *McCall's*. Mark has profiled hundreds of athletes over the last 20 years. He has also written several books about his native New York and New Jersey, his home today. Mark is a graduate of Duke University, with a degree in history. He lives with his daughters and wife, Sarah, overlooking Sandy Hook, NJ.

JAMES L. GATES, JR. has served as Library Director at the National Baseball Hall of Fame since 1995. He had previously served in academic libraries for almost fifteen years. He holds degrees from Belmont Abbey College, the University of Notre Dame and Indiana University. During his career Jim has authored several academic articles and has served in an editorial capacity on multiple book, magazine and museum publications, and he also serves as host for the Annual Cooperstown Symposium on Baseball and American Culture. He is an ardent Baltimore Orioles fan and enjoys watching baseball with his wife and two children.